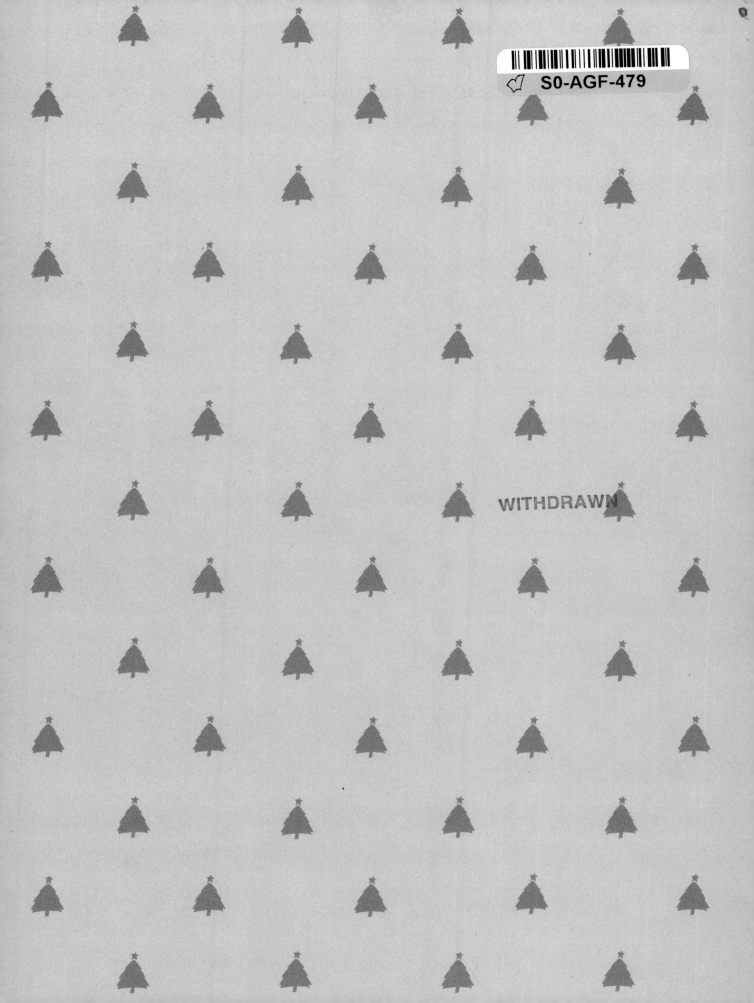

Handmade
CHRISTMAS
Ornaments

Designer and Contributing Writer
Jane Johnston

Publications International, Ltd.

Manufactured in USA

8 7 6 5 4 3 2 1

ISBN 0-7853-0279-4

Photography:
Sacco Productions Limited/Chicago

Photographers:
Ken Hyne, Tom O'Connell, Peter Ross

Photo Stylists:
Linda Banach, Paula Walters

Photo Production:
Roberta Ellis
Models/Royal Model Mangement:
Theresa Lesniak, Monica Magdziak

Jane Johnston is a crafts designer who obtained her Bachelor of Arts
degree in Studio Arts from the University of Pittsburgh. She has sup-
plied many handmade Christmas ornaments to retail stores through-
out southwestern Pennsylvania. Ms. Johnston is also a member of
the Craftsman's Guild of Pittsburgh.

CONTENTS

INTRODUCTION:

VICTORIAN THEME TREE

TEXAS THEME TREE

CHILDREN'S THEME TREE

COUNTRY THEME TREE

INTRODUCTION:
STEPS TO SUCCESS

Crafting handmade Christmas ornaments can be great family fun or an exciting activity for friends of all ages to enjoy. Making your own ornaments can help put the warmth and heart back into a season that, for some, has become "too much." The gift of a handmade ornament says you care enough to spend time on someone special. Give a child an ornament that you have made, and he or she will remember you every time the ornament is hung on a Christmas tree in years to come. For a little something special to give to your friends and neighbors, a handmade ornament is just the right gift.

SOME BASIC TOOLS

Glue. In most cases, white craft glue and hot glue guns can be used interchangeably, but there are differences. White glue takes longer to set up, or establish a bond. Hot glue is better if you don't want to hold something in place for a long time or if you don't want to wait between steps while the glue dries. However, white glue bonds better than hot glue on surfaces that are nonporous (such as a button surface); white glue also bonds better when gluing dissimilar surfaces (nonporous buttons to a porous grapevine).

Since hot glue comes out of the gun in a glob, often some glue will show around the edges of the glued object. In this instance, use a sharp knife or a single-edge razor blade to trim off the excess. By contrast, white glue dries transparent, unless you use extremely large amounts.

When you buy a hot glue gun, consider getting a trigger-action mini gun. Mini guns deliver the smallest amount of glue possible and offer the best control of the nozzle. When using a hot glue gun, let the glue completely cool before getting rid of the annoying "strings" that often appear between the ornament and the hot glue gun. Finally, let the glue cool completely before releasing the glued object; otherwise, the object may shift position.

When you buy white glue, chose one that dries transparent and is specifically made for crafts. The white glue should be flexible, which is an important feature when you are gluing fabric.

Scissors. Although scissors are usually not mentioned in the lists of "What You'll Need," they are necessary for preparing almost every project. Be sure your scissors are sharp; otherwise, cutting felt and polyester batting will be difficult. If possible, try to have one special pair of scissors for cutting fabrics only. Cutting hair or paper dulls the blades quickly.

Orange sticks and toothpicks. An orange stick (from your manicuring kit) is useful for setting rhinestones. With rhinestones or any of the variety of studs available, the main action is pushing the points on the settings through the material and then bending the points over. Although an orange stick takes a bit longer than a setting machine, it will save you money. Toothpicks are useful for almost every project. Toothpicks can be used to spread glue around, to hold things in place, or to push small objects around.

Tweezers. Tweezers are another handy item to keep with your craft tools. They can be used to pick up small objects, such as goggle eyes.

Batting. For felt ornaments, use batting instead of stuffing. Stuffing often develops clumps, especially when it is being pushed into something. Stuffing also never seems to get into the far corners of the ornament.

Paper twist. Paper twist comes in a variety of widths, depending on the manufacturer. Adjust the directions of a project to reflect different widths. Do not cut the paper twist to the size specified in the directions until you have unraveled and spread it as flat as possible.

HANDY TECHNIQUES

Glue. Whenever you are gluing something, it is better to put the glue on the object to be placed (if possible) rather than on the surface where the object will end up. This provides better control and prevents the glue from being smeared.

After cutting the stem from a ribbon rose, apply a dab of hot glue to the rear of the flower. The glue will hold the rose together.

If you are gluing something with a stem, first trim the stem to $1/4$ inch. Apply glue to the $1/4$-inch stem by sticking the stem down the nozzle of the hot glue gun.

To make leaves appear more realistic, apply glue to the bottom rear of the leaves only. This will make them stand up and appear lifelike.

To make it look as if there are more flowers, fruit, gift packages, or bears than actually used, glue the first round of items just peeking above the edge of the object (for example, a sleigh or a cornucopia). Glue the second row to the first row at a slightly higher level. Glue the third row to the second at an even higher level. Make sure there are no holes where someone can see down into the hollow mound you've created.

Ribbon. When choosing a wide ribbon for a bigger project (such as a tree garland), use ribbon with wire in the edge. The wire will help give the ribbon a more graceful line.

If you can't find the ribbon you want in a narrow width, buy wider ribbon and cut it to the width you want.

Beads. Strings of beads usually come with about 6 inches of extra string on either end. To cut a string of beads, make a knot at one end of the string that is large enough that the beads cannot slip off. Move as many inches of beads as you need down against this knot. Tie another knot just past the last bead and cut the string. Place a dab of white glue on each knot to prevent unraveling. (To knot a string in a specific spot, first make a loose knot around a straight pin. Then move the pin to the spot where you want the knot. Tighten the string.)

SOME GENERAL DIRECTIONS

Several directions apply to several projects: making loopy bows, cutting patterns, or tying various knots.

To make a loopy bow:

1. Cut the ribbon to the specified length.

2. Find an object that is approximately the same diameter as the loop of the bow. (Your fingers can work well for this: one for a small loop, two for a larger loop.)

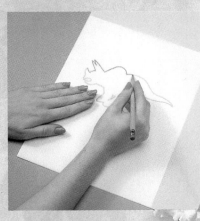

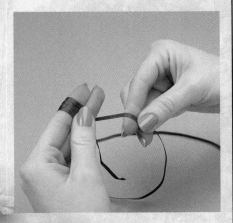

3. Leaving about 1 inch free, wrap the ribbon around the object. Leave another inch free at the end. Cross the two free ends over the loop.

4. Insert a smaller piece of ribbon through all the loops; bring around and tie in a knot.

5. Pull the bow from the object and separate the loops in an attractive arrangement.

To cut out patterns:

1. Place tracing paper over the pattern. Using a pen or pencil, trace the pattern onto the paper.

2. Using rubber cement, bond the tracing paper to a piece of thin cardboard.

3. Cut the shape out, following the traced lines.

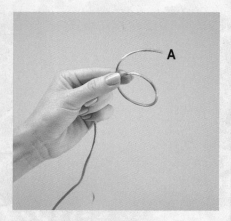

To tie an overhand knot:
1. Create a loop with your line. Note point A .

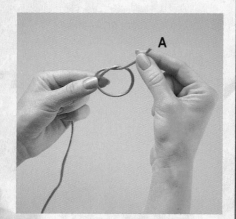

2. Pass point A around and through the loop from behind.

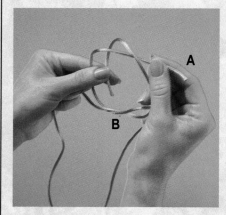

3. Pull the line tight.

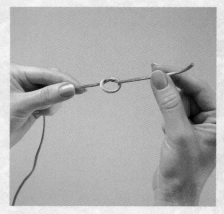

To tie a square knot:

1. Take the two ends of your line, one in each hand. Pass point B over point A.

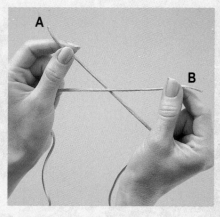

2. Wrap point B around point A, bringing it underneath, up, and out.

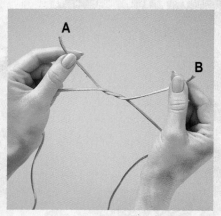

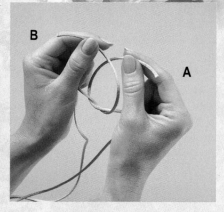

3. Pass point B over point A, forming a loop.

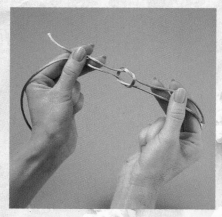

4. Bring point B under point A, then through the loop and out.

5. Pull the line tight with both hands.

THEME TREE IDEAS

Once you've created ornaments for a theme tree, you'll need to think about tree skirts, garlands, and tree toppers to finish decorating your tree.

Victorian Theme Tree. For a tree skirt you can use an old set of lacy curtains. For garlands try 3-inch-wide lace gathered with a bow every 2 to 3 feet. Another option is 3-inch-wide ribbon in a pale color with wire in the edges. A ball of dried or silk flowers with ribbon trailers works well as a tree topper.

Texas Theme Tree. A tree skirt can be made from red and blue bandannas stitched together, or use 3 yards of burlap or cowboy theme fabric. For a garland use several strands of jute twine gathered in a bow every two feet. Small American flags stuck into the sides of the bows might look nice. An alternative garland can be made from bandannas tied together into a string. Make a large star from lightweight aluminum or stitched from burlap to serve as a tree topper.

Children's Theme Tree. Instead of a tree skirt, try piling small stuffed animals around the base of the tree; or, a length of brightly colored flannel would make a fun tree skirt. Use candy for the garland: a string of cellophane-wrapped gumballs or thick red yarn with candy canes tied in every two feet. A tree topper could be created with a loopy bow made from thick red yarn.

Country Theme Tree. For a tree skirt, start with a 3-yard piece of muslin or brown butcher's paper. Next, cut potato stamps in basic shapes and then stamp the material using acrylic paint. A strand of jute twine works well as a garland. Gather the twine in a bow every two feet; stick bright red berries or a holly pick in each side of the bow. You can also use jute twine to make the tree topper: Make a thick loopy bow from the twine.

HOW DIFFICULT IS EACH ORNAMENT?

The ornament projects vary in difficulty. Many are easy; many are intermediate; and some are difficult. Most of the projects have been designed to be as simple as possible. The easy projects are best suited for beginners. The intermediate and difficult projects use many of the same skills called for in the easy projects, but there are more steps and more parts to put together.

Victorian Theme Tree
Beaded Wreath: easy
Cornucopia of Roses: easy
Hats Off to the Holidays: easy
Royal Yule Ornament: intermediate
Snow Bird: intermediate
Victorian Angel: difficult

Texas Theme Tree
Festive Bolo: easy
Holly Badge: easy
Pepper Yule Party: easy
Red-Hot Wreath: easy
Cowgirl Hat: intermediate
Christmas Kerchief: intermediate
On the Christmas Trail: intermediate
Texas Santa: intermediate

Children's Theme Tree
Bears on a Sleigh Ride: easy
Christmas Olé: easy
Pom-Pom Snowman: easy
Dinosaur in December: intermediate
Noel Rocking Horse: intermediate

Country Theme Tree
Buttons 'n' Eyelet Wreath: easy
Old-Fashioned Buttermold: easy
Country Christmas Goose: intermediate
Holiday Holstein: intermediate
Jute Twist: intermediate
Old World St. Nick: difficult

Individual Ornaments
And a Partridge in a...: easy
Braided Candy Cane: easy
Dove of Peace: easy
Joy to the World: easy
Santa's Sleigh: easy
Angel of the Vine: intermediate
Cross-Stitch Christmas: intermediate
O Christmas Tree!: intermediate
Bountiful Santa: difficult
Button-Down Santa: difficult
Jolly Clay Santa: difficult
Yuletide Bauble: difficult

VICTORIAN THEME TREE

❧

*Imagine yourself
in an earlier time; catch
the feeling
of Christmas past
with a Victorian
theme tree.
Cornucopias, lace,
and pastels will bring
the look and feel
of this refined era
to all your Christmas
celebrations. Turn to
the Introduction for
ideas on Victorian
garlands,
skirts, and topppers.*

ROYAL YULE ORNAMENT

1. Cut out the pattern. See page 64 for the "Royal Yule Ornament" pattern. See Introduction, page 5, for directions on cutting out patterns. Cut, on the bias, 7 pattern pieces from the blue fabric.

2. Attach the 7 pieces of fabric to the foam ball with pins. The pieces should be evenly distributed around the ball and overlap slightly.

3. Cover the overlapping fabric edges with the 7 lengths of gold trim. Secure with pins and spot glue in place. Remove the pins after the glue has dried.

4. Glue a 3½-inch length of gold trim in a circle to the top of the ball and another to the bottom.

5. Glue the tassel to the center of the bottom circle of gold trim.

6. Place the 24-inch length of blue ribbon on top of the 24-inch length of gold ribbon. Make a 1-inch-diameter loopy bow. Tie off the bow with the 8-inch length of blue ribbon. (See Introduction, page 5, for instructions on making a loopy bow.) Glue the bow to the center of the top circle of gold trim.

7. Fold the 8-inch length of gold ribbon in half and tie an overhand knot near the open end. Glue the folded end near the loopy bow.

WHAT YOU'LL NEED

12-inch-square blue fabric
Scissors
3-inch-diameter foam ball
Sequin pins
7 lengths antique gold trim, 4¾ inches each
Hot glue mini gun
2 lengths antique gold trim, 3½ inches each
5-inch gold tinsel tassel
24 inches blue ⅛-inch ribbon
24 inches gold ⅛-inch ribbon
8 inches blue ⅛-inch ribbon
8 inches gold ⅛-inch ribbon

TIPS AND VARIATIONS

Give this ornament a Texas or Western look by using a bandanna for the material. Use jute twine for the trim and tassel.

CORNUCOPIA OF ROSES

1. Starting at the lowest point of the mouth of the cone, weave the 9-inch length of ¹/₁₆-inch ribbon around the edge. Trim any excess ribbon and glue the ends in place.

2. Mix together the light and dark mauve rosebuds. Twist the stems together and, about 2 inches from the bottom of the flowers, bend the stems back on themselves. If necessary, clip the stems to a total length of 3 inches.

3. Insert arrangement into cone. Glue one rose on each side and top and bottom to edge of cone.

4. Clip the stems from the rose leaves. One at a time, apply glue to the bottom of the leaves and insert them into the flower bouquet in an attractive arrangement.

5. Lay the 18-inch lengths of ribbon on top of each other. Make a 2-inch bow and glue it to the lower side of the open end of the cone, just below the flower arrangement.

6. Fold the 12-inch length of ribbon in half. Make an overhand knot near the open end. Glue the folded end just below the 2-inch bow.

TIPS AND VARIATIONS

For variety, use miniature poinsettias in pastel colors.

WHAT YOU'LL NEED

5-inch crochet cone
9 inches ¹/₁₆-inch mauve ribbon
Scissors
Hot glue mini gun
1 bunch (6 flowers) ³/₄-inch dark mauve, brushed gold rosebuds
1 bunch (6 flowers) ³/₄-inch light mauve, brushed gold rosebuds
Wire cutters
9 rose leaves, ¹/₂-inch leaves
3 lengths ¹/₁₆-inch mauve ribbon, 18 inches each
12 inches ¹/₁₆-inch mauve ribbon

Hats Off to the Holidays

1. Glue the 8-mm beads around base of crown of the crochet hat.

2. Clip the wires off the glass ball picks. Glue the picks in a clump of three at the crown's base, next to the 8-mm beads.

3. Clip the stems from the leaves. Glue the leaves in an attractive arrangement next to the glass picks.

4. Make a ¾-inch-diameter loopy bow from one 15-inch length of mauve ribbon. Tie off the loopy bow with the second length of 15-inch mauve ribbon. Trim ends. (See Introduction, page 5, for instructions on making a loopy bow.) Glue the bow to the glass picks.

5. Fold the 20-inch length of ribbon in half. Insert it through the edge of the hat brim almost opposite to the glass picks. Tie an overhand knot near the end.

Tips and Variations

Ribbon roses could be used in place of the beads, with larger roses in place of the glass ball picks.

What You'll Need

4-inch crochet hat
22 clear beads, 8 mm each
Hot glue mini gun
Wire cutters
3 glass ball picks, 15 mm each
2 rose leaves, ½ inch each
2 lengths mauve ⅛-inch ribbon, 15 inches each
20 inches mauve 1/16-inch ribbon

SNOW BIRD

1. Remove the tape from the bottom of the cage. Slip knife between the cage bottom and edge. Pop out the bottom.

2. Pick up one end of the bead string with tweezers. Apply hot glue to the last bead. Reach inside the cage and hold that bead against the center top of the cage until the glue dries. Repeat with the other end of the bead string.

3. Clip off the wires that stick out from the bottom of the bird. Prop the cage partially upright and hot glue the bird to the middle of the bead string. (Use tweezers to hold the bead string still.)

4. Pop the cage bottom back into place.

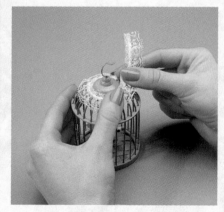

5. Apply a thin line of white glue to the back upper edge of the 5½-inch length of lace. Place the lace on the wicker bars of the cage just below the solid piece of wood at the cage's top. Trim the lace to overlap ¼ inch. Let dry.

What You'll Need

3½-inch wicker bird cage
Paring knife
5-inch string blue 3-mm beads
Tweezers
Hot glue mini gun
2-inch dove
Wire cutters
White craft glue
5½ inches ½-inch lace
4 inches ½-inch lace
4 inches blue ⅛-inch ribbon
8½ inches ½-inch lace
8½ inches blue ⅛-inch ribbon
2 lengths blue ⅛-inch ribbon,
18 inches each

6. Apply a thin line of white glue to the edge of the solid piece of wood above the lace from step 5 at the cage's top. Place the 4-inch length of lace around this edge. Trim the lace to overlap ¼ inch. Let dry.

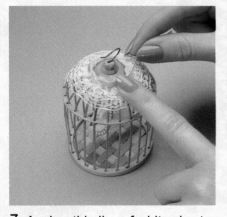

7. Apply a thin line of white glue to the upper edge of the lace from step 6. Place the 4-inch length of blue ribbon over the glue. Trim any extra ribbon.

8. Locate the solid piece of wood through which the bars pass (about 2½ inches from the bottom of the cage). Apply a thin line of white glue to this piece. Attach the 8½-inch length of lace here. Trim the lace to overlap ¼ inch. Let dry.

9. Apply a thin line of white glue to the upper edge of the lace from step 8. Place the 8½-inch length of blue ribbon over the glue. Trim any extra ribbon.

10. Lay the 18-inch lengths of ribbon on top of each other. Make a 2-inch bow. Hot glue the bow to the cage's top, at the bottom of the hook.

TIPS AND VARIATIONS

Fill the cage with a bouquet of silk rosebuds instead of a bird.

Victorian Angel

What You'll Need

3 lengths pale blue 3½-inch-wide paper twist for under-skirt and under-blouse, 3 inches each

3 lengths 3½-inch-wide pattern paper twist for over-skirt and over-blouse, 3 inches each

12 inches 3½-inch-wide pattern paper twist for wings

Hot glue mini gun

Scissors

1-inch-diameter wooden angel head

Wood wool

3 lengths off-white ⅛-inch ribbon, 18 inches each

18 inches pale blue ⅛-inch ribbon

6 inches off-white ⅛-inch ribbon

8 inches pale blue ⅛-inch ribbon

---

1. Untwist and flatten all paper twist.

UNDER-SKIRT AND OVER-SKIRT:

1. Run a thin line of glue down the right 3-inch side of one of the pieces of pale blue paper. Place the left 3-inch side of a second piece of pale blue paper over the glue of the first piece of pale blue paper, creating a 3-inch by 7½-inch rectangle.

2. Run a thin line of glue down the left 3-inch side of the rectangle. Bend the right 3-inch side of the rectangle around to overlap the glue line, forming a tube.

3. Gather together one end of the tube. Apply glue to the gathered end, forming a cone. This is the under-skirt.

4. To start making the over-skirt, round off the corners of a 3-inch side of 2 of the 3-inch pieces of pattern paper twist.

5. Gather together the square corners of each pattern piece. Glue the gathered end of each pattern piece to opposite sides of the top of the under-skirt. Be sure the squared ends of the two pattern pieces overlap.

UNDER-BLOUSE AND OVER-BLOUSE:

1. Run a thin line of glue down both 3½-inch sides of the third piece of pale blue paper. (This will be the under-blouse.) Place the third pattern piece of paper on top of the blue paper, pattern side up. (This will be the over-blouse.)

2. Fold the under-blouse and over-blouse in half, bringing the glued sides together. The pattern piece (over-blouse) should be on top.

3. Gather the glued sides together. Apply glue to the gathered end.

ANGEL'S BODY:

1. To join the skirt and blouse, apply glue to the tip of the skirt. Place the gathered end of the blouse on the glue and hold until the glue cools.

2. Pull the pale blue paper of the shoulders out further than the pattern paper. Be sure the shoulders are rolled, not folded.

3. Glue the angel's head to the center of the shoulders.

4. Mold a 2-inch-diameter clump of wood wool to a hair shape.

5. Apply glue to the hair area of the head. Attach the wood wool to the head.

6. To make the belt, fold 2 lengths of the 18-inch off-white ribbon in half. Apply glue to the back center of the waist and attach the folded ends of the ribbons.

7. Bring both ribbons around to the angel's front. Tie a 1½-inch bow at the front center of the waist.

ANGEL'S WINGS:

1. To make the wings, fold the 12-inch length of pattern paper in half, bringing the 3½-inch sides together. Open up. Run a thin line of glue down the center line.

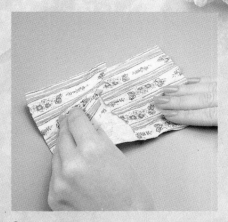

2. Fold in the right half, placing the 3½-inch end on the glue line. Run another thin line of glue down the center line. Fold in the left half, placing the 3½-inch end on the glue line.

3. Gather the paper together at the center line, forming wings.

4. Apply glue to the back center of the blouse and attach the wings.

FINISHING:

1. Place the third 18-inch length of off-white ribbon on top of the 18-inch-length of pale blue ribbon. Make a 1-inch-diameter loopy bow. Tie off the bow with the 6-inch length of ribbon. (See Introduction, page 5, for instructions on making a loopy bow.)

2. Glue bow to the top of the hair.

3. Fold the 8-inch length of ribbon in half. Glue the open end to the base of the bow.

BEADED WREATH

WHAT YOU'LL NEED

3-inch bleached grapevine wreath
22-inch string mauve 3-mm beads
22-inch string blue 3-mm beads
Hot glue mini gun
Wire cutters
3 blue ribbon roses, ¼ inch each
2 rose leaves, ½ inch each
18 inches blue ⅛-inch ribbon
2 lengths mauve 1/16-inch ribbon,
18 inches each
12 inches blue ⅛-inch ribbon

1. Glue one end of both bead strings to the rear of the wreath.

2. Wrap both strings of beads around the wreath. Finish by gluing the ends of both strings to the rear of the wreath where the strings were first glued.

3. Clip the stems from the roses and leaves. Glue them to the front of the wreath between two rows of beads.

4. Place the 18-inch length of blue ribbon on top of the two lengths of mauve ribbon. Make a 2-inch bow. Glue the bow to the top of the wreath. (The roses and leaves should be positioned at the lower right of the wreath.)

5. Fold the 12-inch length of blue ribbon in half and tie an overhand knot near the open end. Glue the folded end just behind the bow.

TIPS AND VARIATIONS

Slip some narrow lace under the edges of the beads.

Fabric stores stock many special trims for the holiday season only. Look through the seasonal bins for a special trim that strikes your fancy.

Choose a color combination that matches your bedroom and hang this ornament on the wall after your tree comes down.

O CHRISTMAS TREE!

1. Cut out the pattern for "O Christmas Tree!" See page 64 for the pattern. See Introduction, page 5, for instructions on cutting out patterns.

2. Place the pattern on the wrong side of the green material. Trace the pattern on the material; cut out the tree figure, allowing a ¼-inch seam allowance. Repeat once with the green material and once with one thickness of batting.

3. Place the right sides of the two tree figures together. Place the batting on top of the green material.

4. Sew the batting and the two tree figures together, leaving an opening at the base of the tree. Sew again, to reinforce the seams.

7. Attach the garland to the tree by spot basting on the seams. (If you have garland left over, apply a spot of glue to the knot at the end of the nylon line and attach to the tree.)

8. Baste the ornaments onto the tree in a random pattern.

5. Trim the seams and clip the curves of the tree.

6. Turn the tree right side out. Baste the opening shut.

9. Cover the basting by gluing ½-inch bows over the knots.

10. Fold the 9-inch length of red ribbon in half. Glue the open end to the tree top.

11. Make a 1¼-inch bow from the 12-inch length of red ribbon. Glue over the glued end of the ribbon in step 10.

WHAT YOU'LL NEED

2 swatches green pattern material, 6-inch squares
Pen or pencil
Scissors
6-inch square polyester batting
Sewing machine
Thread to match the green material
1 yard of mini-garland
Needle
4 wooden mini-ornaments
4 gold mini-ornaments, 8 mm each
3 gold mini-ornaments, 6 mm each
White craft glue
11 red bows, ⅜ inch each
(or 18 inches of red ¹⁄₁₆-inch ribbon to make bows)
9 inches red ¹⁄₁₆-inch ribbon
12 inches red ¼-inch ribbon

BUTTON-DOWN SANTA

Buttons are hot and this Santa has plenty of them. Hang Button-Down Santa on your tree or on a doorknob, or sit him on the mantle to greet your children on Christmas morning.

WHAT YOU'LL NEED

Scissors

12-inch-square swatch red felt

Matching red thread for sewing machine

12-inch-square swatch black felt

Matching black thread for sewing machine

12-inch-square swatch muslin

Matching off-white thread for sewing machine

12-inch-square swatch burlap

Matching beige thread for sewing machine

Pins

Sewing machine

Polyester fiberfill

Needle

2 spools extra-strong cream-color thread; we used Coats Dual Duty Extra Strong #116

1 spool black thread; we used Coats Dual Duty Extra Strong, Black

70 or more buttons; two holes, various colors (white, off-white, black, and red), and various sizes (mostly 3/8 inch, some 3/4 inch)

Permanent black marker

15 inches jute twine, for sack

Permanent red marker

Pencil

Red embroidery thread (321 DMC)

Blue embroidery thread (312 DMC)

White craft glue

2 lengths jute twine, for legs, 7 inches each

24 inches jute twine, for hanger and bow

1. Cut out all patterns. See pages 62–63 for the "Button-Down Santa" patterns. See Introduction, page 5, for directions on cutting out patterns. Allow a 1/4-inch seam allowance for sewing.

2. Place the suit and hat patterns on the red felt and cut 2 Santa's suits, 2 hats, and 2 hatbands. Place the boot pattern on the black felt and cut 4 boots. Place the body pattern on the muslin and cut 2 bodies. Cut an 8-inch by 3 1/2-inch piece from the burlap.

SANTA'S SUIT:

1. Fold both pieces of red felt along the fold lines (indicated on the pattern) at the lower edge. Pin in place.

2. Using the matching red thread, sew along sew line A (indicated on the pattern) for all four corners.

3. With the right sides of the red felt pieces together, sew the front and back together along sew line B, leaving the sleeves and neck open. (See the pattern for location of sewing lines.)

4. Clip the corners. Turn the suit right side out. Stuff the suit three-quarters full with polyester fiberfill.

SANTA'S BODY:

1. Place the right sides of the 2 pieces of muslin together. Using matching thread, sew along the sew lines (indicated on the pattern), leaving the bottom edge open.

2. Clip the curves. Turn the body right side out. Stuff the body with polyester fiberfill. Baste the lower edge shut.

3. Compress and slide the bottom of Santa's body into the suit through the neck.

4. Thread the needle with about 20 inches extra-strong cream-color thread, doubled. Tie an overhand knot about 2 inches from the ends.

5. Take a running stitch about 3/16 inch from the edge of the neck on Santa's suit. Pull the thread to gather the suit's neck close to the body's neck. Tie off the thread and trim any excess.

SANTA'S HAT:

1. Sew (using matching red thread) one of Santa's hatbands to the lower edge of Santa's hat, wrong sides together. Do the same for the other hatband and hat.

2. Put the 2 hats on top of each other, wrong sides together. Sew (using matching red thread) only the hatband edges together.

3. Turn the hat so the right sides are together and sew (using matching red thread) the rest of the hat together.

4. Turn the hat right side out. Turn the hatband up 3/4 inch. The seam connecting the hatband to the hat should not show.

5. Thread the needle with extra-strong cream-color thread, doubled. Tie a knot 1/4 inch from the ends. Insert the needle along the hatband and pull through about 1/4 inch away from the original insertion. Tie a knot next to the hatband and clip the thread to 1/4 inch. Repeat until hatband is filled with many knots. The knot arrangement is random and occasionally interspersed with the extra-strong black thread and knots.

Button-Down Santa

6. To make the tassel, thread needle with extra-strong cream-color thread, doubled. Draw the needle through the hat's peak. Leave about 1½ inches of thread hanging free on either side of the peak. Repeat until tassel is full.

Santa's boots:

1. Place the boots with the right sides together. Using matching black thread, sew the boots together along the sew line (indicated in the pattern). Leave the tops of the boots open.

2. Clip the curves. Turn the boots right side out. Stuff each boot with polyester fiberfill.

3. Thread the needle with about 20 inches extra-strong black thread, doubled. Make an overhand knot about 2 inches from the ends. Take a running stitch about ³/₁₆ inch from the upper edge of the boot. Pull the thread to gather the top of the boot shut. Tie off the thread and trim any excess.

Santa's legs:

1. Thread the needle with about 20 inches extra-strong cream-color thread, doubled. Tie an overhand knot near the ends; clip excess thread to ⅛ inch.

2. Insert the needle into the side of a boot and up through the center of the gathering. Begin threading buttons for the legs. Start with a ¾-inch button to cover the top of the boot. Place a ¾-inch red button about 1¼ inches up the stack.

3. When the stack of buttons reaches about 2½ inches, insert the needle into Santa's bottom about ½ inch in from Santa's side. Bring the needle back out of Santa's bottom about ¼ inch away.

4. Take the thread back down the stack of buttons, through the second hole in each button. Insert the needle down through the center of the boot's gathering and out the side of the boot, just below gathering stitch. Allow a little room on the thread to add a jute twine bow later. Knot the thread and clip any excess. Use the black marker to color any thread that shows around the top of the boot.

5. Repeat for Santa's other leg.

Santa's sack:

1. Fold the burlap in half, bringing the 3½-inch sides together.

2. Using the matching thread, sew the sides together, leaving the top of the sack open.

3. Turn the sack inside out and stuff about three-quarters full with polyester fiberfill.

4. Gather the top of the sack about 1 inch from the opening. Wrap the 15-inch length of twine around the gathering and tie a 2 ¾-inch bow.

Santa's arms:

1. Thread the needle with about 20 inches of extra-strong cream-color thread, doubled. Tie a knot near the ends and clip excess thread to ⅛ inch.

2. Insert the needle into the cuff of Santa's suit about ³/₁₆ inch from the edge. Take a running stitch around the cuff. Pull the thread to gather the cuff. Tie off the thread, but do not cut it.

3. Begin threading buttons for the arms. Start with a ¾-inch white button; follow with a ¾-inch red button.

4. When about 1 inch of buttons have been threaded, insert the needle through the gathered area of Santa's sack and out the other side. String buttons in reverse order for Santa's other arm.

5. Insert the needle into the second cuff about 3/16 inch from the edge. Take a running stitch around the cuff. Pull the thread to gather the cuff. Tie off the thread, but do not cut it.

6. Insert the needle back through the second hole in each button, through the sack, and through the second group of buttons.

7. Insert the needle through the gathered material at the cuff and out below the gathering stitches. Knot the thread and clip off any excess. Use the red marker to color any thread that shows around the gathering at the cuffs.

SANTA'S FACE:

1. With the pencil, draw Santa's lower lip and mark the eye placement (indicated on the pattern).

2. Use the red embroidery thread to satin stitch Santa's lower lip. Use the blue embroidery thread to stitch French knots for Santa's eyes.

3. To make Santa's hair, moustache, and beard, thread the needle with extra-strong cream-color thread. Insert the needle into Santa's head and take a 1/4-inch stitch, leaving about 2 inches hanging free on either side of the stitch. (Do not tie any knots.)

4. Repeat until the hair and beard are thick. When finished, trim the thread to shape the hair and beard. For the moustache, trim the hanging ends to 1/2 inch.

FINISHING:

1. Apply white craft glue to the inside rim of Santa's hat. Place the hat on Santa's head with the seams to each side. Hold until the glue sets.

2. To make the leg bows, wrap the 7-inch lengths of jute twine around the legs just above the 3/4-inch button next to the boots. Tie a 1 1/2-inch bow.

3. Fold the 24-inch length of jute twine in half. Knot the twine around the base of the tassel about 5 inches down from the folded end. Tie a 2-inch bow with the remaining twine. Trim the ends to 2 inches.

4. Apply a dab of white glue to the back of the twine and tassel so the knot won't slip off. Let dry.

TIPS AND VARIATIONS

If you fill Santa's bottom with dried beans, he will sit on your mantle.

Texas
Theme
Tree

*Put a new and
different spin on your
Christmas celebration
by selecting a
Texas theme for
your tree. Decorate
your tree with unique
ornaments that say
Lone Star State:
bandannas, cowboys,
longhorn steers,
and more. You can
complete your Texas tree
with pointers on garlands,
toppers, and skirts from
the Introduction.*

HOLLY BADGE

WHAT YOU'LL NEED

½-inch brush
2-inch 5-pointed wooden star
Acrylic paints: yellow and black
5/0 red sable brush
Wire cutters
2 holly leaves, ½-inch leaves
⅛-inch stamen
Hot glue mini gun
2 inches red ⅛-inch ribbon
8 inches gold elastic cord

1. Using the ½-inch brush, paint both sides of the star yellow.

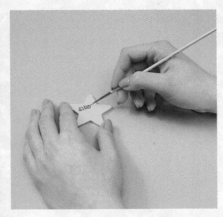

2. Using the 5/0 red sable brush, paint "Sheriff" in black.

3. Trim the stems from the holly leaves and the stamen. Glue the leaves and stamen on the star at the lower right of the star.

4. Make a ¾-inch bow from the ribbon. Glue the bow just above the holly leaves.

5. Fold the gold cord in half. Tie an overhand knot near the open end. Glue the knot to the rear of the star's top point.

TIPS AND VARIATIONS

You don't have to use a 5-pointed star; in the old West, sheriff badges came in many shapes and sizes. There were also U.S. Marshals and Texas Rangers in the old West; make an entire collection!

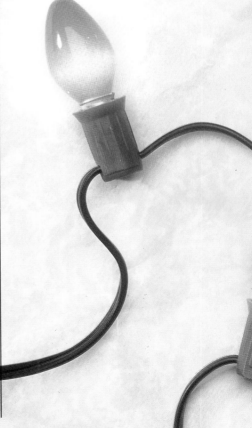

TEXAS SANTA

WHAT YOU'LL NEED

Scissors
Felt squares: red, white, black, and gold
Pen or pencil
Chalk
White craft glue
Polyester craft batting
Wire cutters
2 holly leaves, ½-inch leaves
Hot glue mini gun
⅛-inch stamen
10 inches gold thread
Needle

1. Cut out all patterns. See page 61 for the "Texas Santa" patterns. See Introduction, page 5, for directions on cutting out patterns.

2. Place the patterns on the felt: red for the main figure and lips; white for the chaps, cuffs, beard, hatband, and hat pom-pom; black for the belt; and gold for the belt buckle. Trace the patterns onto the felt with a pen or pencil (use chalk for the black felt).

3. Following the lines traced on the red felt, cut out the main figure. The side showing the lines will be called the wrong side. Cut out the lips from the red felt. Following the lines traced on the white, black, and gold felt squares, cut out the chaps, cuffs, beard, hatband, hat pom-pom, belt, and belt buckle.

4. Glue the following pieces in place using white craft glue: hat pom-pom, hatband, beard, lips, belt, belt buckle, chaps, and cuffs. Let dry.

5. Place the pattern of the main figure on the black felt. Outline the general shape using chalk. Allow at least ½ inch outside the main figure (don't forget to include room for the chaps).

6. Cut out the general shape from the black felt.

7. Place the pattern of the main figure on one thickness of batting. Trace the general shape with a pen or pencil.

24

8. Move ¼ inch inside the tracing and cut out the figure.

9. On the wrong side of the figure, run a thin line of white craft glue around the edge.

10. Place the batting on top of the wrong side of the figure and inside the line of glue.

11. Pick up the figure and batting; be sure not to touch the glue or let the batting slip.

12. Place the figure and batting on top of the black felt from step 6. Press the edges of the figure onto the black felt. Continue pressing until the glue sets and the figure sticks to the black felt. Set aside until glue dries (about 20 minutes).

13. Trim the black felt to within ⅛ inch of the figure.

14. Trim the stems from the holly leaves and glue to the hat using hot glue.

15. Glue the stamen on the holly leaves using hot glue.

16. Double thread the needle with gold thread. Draw the needle through the pom-pom.

17. Tie an overhand knot about 4 inches above the figure. Cut off any excess thread.

TIPS AND VARIATIONS

Try tracing the pattern on ¼-inch-thick basswood, available at hobby shops. Then use a scroll saw to cut out the ornament. Paint the wood in your favorite colors with acrylic paints.

Instead of glue, sew the figure to the black felt backing using a fancy stitch in a contrasting color thread.

ON THE CHRISTMAS TRAIL

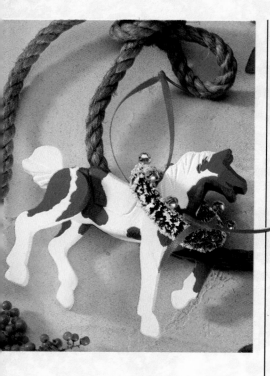

WHAT YOU'LL NEED

Carved horse, 4 inches by 3½ inches
½-inch brush
Acrylic paints: white and brown
8 inches red ⅛-inch ribbon
2-inch frosted sisal wreath
White craft glue
5 inches red ⅛-inch ribbon
Tweezers
7 jingle bells, 6 mm each

1. Cover the entire horse with two coats of white paint.

2. Apply brown pinto markings.

3. Slip the 8-inch length of ribbon through the wreath and tie an overhand knot about ½ inch from the open end. Reshape the wreath from a circle into an oval.

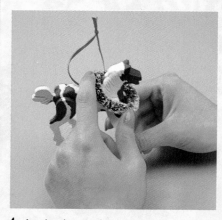

4. Apply glue at the bottom of the horse's mane. Slip the wreath over the horse's head, placing the ribbon in the glue. Hold the wreath and ribbon in place until the glue sets.

5. Make a ¾-inch bow with the 5-inch length of ribbon. Glue to the wreath on the right front side.

6. Using the tweezers, glue the jingle bells evenly around the wreath.

TIPS AND VARIATIONS

Paint the horse to match your favorite breed; an encyclopedia will have photographs of many breeds of horses. Painting the horse turquoise and pink will give you a horse with a Southwestern style.

Pepper Yule Party

1. Braid three peppers together.

2. In the second row, add a pepper each time you twist one of the three braiding wires from the first row (French braid). Continue adding peppers.

3. After all 12 peppers have been braided in, continue braiding the wires together.

4. Bend the braided wire behind the peppers to form a hook.

5. Using the 18-inch lengths of red and green ribbon, make a 3-inch bow. Glue the bow to the top of the peppers.

6. Insert the red and green 8-inch lengths of ribbon through the braided wire hook. Tie an overhand knot 1 inch from the open ends.

What You'll Need

12 plastic red peppers, 7/8 inch each
18 inches red 1/8-inch ribbon
18 inches green 1/8-inch ribbon
Hot glue mini gun
8 inches red 1/8-inch ribbon
8 inches green 1/8-inch ribbon

Tips and Variations

You can make a nice arrangement for your front door by using much larger red peppers.

In many European countries, it is traditional to hang fruit and sometimes vegetables on a Christmas tree. You can create a similar effect using miniature fruits and vegetables. Just be sure there are wires to braid.

If the red coating on the peppers chips, red fingernail polish works as a great touch-up.

CHRISTMAS KERCHIEF

WHAT YOU'LL NEED

Iron

1 standard 18-inch-square red bandanna

2 glazed 3-leaved holly picks, ¾-inch leaves

Hot glue mini gun

8 gold-brushed alder cones

8 inches red ⅛-inch ribbon

Red thread

Needle

1. Iron the bandanna flat. Fold and iron the plain border underneath so that only the design area shows.

2. Fold the bandanna into a triangular shape. Iron flat again.

3. Fold the long edge up ½ inch. Continue folding in same direction until about 2 inches remain unfolded at the tip of the bandanna.

4. The tip should be at the center of the folded bandanna. Fold the bandanna in half, using the tip as the center. Tie a square knot about 4 inches from the center tip.

5. Pull the ends of the bandanna out from the square knot. Iron the ends flat.

6. Insert a holly pick into each side of the knot. Shoot a little hot glue into each side to hold the holly in place.

7. Arrange the alder cones into two groups of four. Apply hot glue to the stems of one group and place it in on one side of the knot. Repeat for the other side.

8. Fold the ribbon in half and tie an overhand knot near the open end. Sew the folded end to the back of the square knot.

TIPS AND VARIATIONS

Bandannas come in many colors. A turquoise or pink bandanna provides a Southwestern-style ornament.

1. Fold the 20-inch length of leather in half. Make sure colored sides of the leather are up and flat.

2. Starting at the top rear of the bolo, thread at least 3½ inches of the open end through the openings in the bolo.

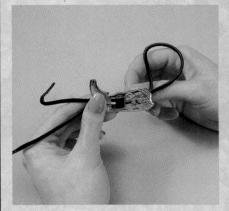

3. Again starting at the top rear of the bolo, thread the 1-inch length of leather into the bolo openings between the strands of the 20-inch piece. Trim any excess at the top or bottom of the bolo.

What You'll Need

20 inches ⅛-inch-wide leather
2-inch bolo
1 inch ⅛-inch-wide leather

Tips and Variations

Bolos come in many different metals and shapes. When choosing additional shapes, be sure the leather will feed through the bolo's holes.

COWGIRL HAT

WHAT YOU'LL NEED

12 inches tricolor 4-mm cord
4-inch white Stetson
Hot glue mini gun
14 rhinestone settings, 4-mm size
7 green rhinestones, 4 mm each
7 red rhinestones, 4 mm each
Orange stick
8 inches gold elastic cord

1. Fold the tricolor cord in half. Glue the halfway point to the side of the hat crown.

2. Loosely cross the cord on the other side of the crown and glue in place.

3. Trim the ends of the cord so they overhang the hat brim by ⅛ inch. Glue the ends to the hat brim.

4. Push the points of a rhinestone setting through the hat brim from underneath to the top. Place a rhinestone into the points.

5. Using the orange stick, push the points over the rhinestone to hold it in place. Repeat until all rhinestones have been placed around the brim, alternating red and green rhinestones.

6. Fold the elastic cord in half and tie an overhand knot about an inch from the open end. Glue the knot to the bottom front edge of the brim.

TIPS AND VARIATIONS

For variety, use miniature felt cowboy/cowgirl hats in different colors or shapes. You can also vary the look by choosing studs other than rhinestones. Instead of tricolor cord, glue lace around the brim for a more feminine look.

Red-Hot Wreath

1. Make a ⅞-inch bow from the 3-inch length of ribbon.

2. Trim the stems from the red peppers. Glue in place on the wreath.

3. Glue the bow in place just above the peppers.

4. Insert the 10-inch length of ribbon through the center of the wreath. Match the ends of the ribbon, then put a dab of glue on the top rear of the wreath to fix the ribbon in place. Tie an overhand knot 3 inches above the wreath. Make a 1½-inch bow above the overhand knot.

What You'll Need

3 inches green ⅛-inch ribbon
3 plastic red peppers, ⅞ inch each
Wire cutters
3-inch-diameter grapevine wreath
Hot glue mini gun
10 inches green ⅛-inch ribbon

JOLLY CLAY SANTA

1. Start Santa's head with a basic 2-inch egg shape in #02 FIMO. Add small balls and "snakes" to build up the forehead, nose, cheeks, and eyes. Use toothpicks as well as your fingers to place the balls and snakes; use the paring knife to refine Santa's face.

2. Snip off the small end of a paper clip. Push about half of the remaining "U" shape into the top of Santa's head, open end facing down.

3. Using the rolling pin, roll a snake ⅛-inch diameter by ⅜-inch length from the #29 FIMO. Shape into an arc and place about ¼ inch below Santa's nose. This will be Santa's lower lip.

4. Roll about 25 snakes, ⅛-inch diameter, from #0 FIMO. Press one end of each snake onto the face and drape gracefully to form the beard. Taper the beard ends with your fingertips.

5. Roll four snakes from the #0 FIMO. The snakes should be about ¾ inch long, starting with a diameter of ⅛ inch and tapering to a point. Press two onto the face above the lips for Santa's mustache; press two above the eyes for Santa's eyebrows.

WHAT YOU'LL NEED

#02 FIMO, face color
Toothpicks
Paring knife
Wire cutters
Paper clip
Rolling pin
#29 FIMO, red
#0 FIMO, white
5/0 red sable brush
Acrylic paints: white and blue
Baking sheet
½-inch brush
FIMO water-based gloss varnish
8 inches white ⅛-inch ribbon

6. Using the rolling pin, roll out a shape from the #29 FIMO that is about 2½ inches by 4 inches and ⅛ inch thick. Use the paring knife to cut a triangle with a 2½-inch base. This will be Santa's hat.

7. Drape and press the base of the triangle across Santa's forehead. Pull the tip of the triangle down to the side of the base.

8. Make about 34 balls of several different sizes from #0 FIMO. Press them in a random arrangement along the bottom ½ inch of the hat's base. These will form the white cuff of Santa's hat.

9. Make several more balls from #0 FIMO. Press these on the tip of Santa's hat.

10. Paint Santa's eyes white using the 5/0 brush and the white acrylic paint. Let dry. Mix a small amount of the white and blue acrylic paints together to create a light blue color. Paint the iris of Santa's eyes light blue. Let dry. Paint Santa's pupils dark blue, using only the blue acrylic paint.

11. Move the ornament to a baking sheet. (You may want to use a spatula to move the ornament.) Bake at 200 degrees Fahrenheit for 2 hours. Let cool.

12. Using the ½-inch brush, paint the ornament with FIMO water-based gloss varnish. Let dry 24 hours.

13. Thread the 8-inch length of white ribbon through the paper clip. Tie an overhand knot near the open end.

TIPS AND VARIATIONS

You can make many Christmas ornaments from FIMO clay; let your imagination run wild.

A low temperature and long baking time were used because Santa's head has a lot of white color and the egg shape is so thick. Don't hurry the baking process by turning the oven to a high temperature; this will cause scorching and burning. Generally, the longer the FIMO clay is baked, the stronger it will be.

ANGEL OF THE VINE

WHAT YOU'LL NEED

2 lengths iridescent 3½-inch-wide
paper twist, 5 inches each

Hot glue mini gun

5-inch gold grape spray

⅝-inch diameter wooden angel
head (with drilled hole)

Wood wool

3 holly leaves, 1½ inches each

Wire cutters

18 inches white, gold edged
½-inch ribbon

8 inches white ⅛-inch ribbon

---

1. Untwist and open the paper twist.
Fold each in half, bringing the 3½-inch
sides together.

2. Gather the open ends together.
Glue the gathered ends. These will be
the angel's wings.

3. Glue the gathered ends of the wings
to the backside of the grape spray
stem.

4. Slip the head down the grape stem
until it sits on top of the wings. Glue
the head in place.

5. Compress about a 1-inch-diameter
clump of wood wool. Apply glue to the
hair area of the angel's head. Arrange
wood wool on top of the angel's head
around the stem.

6. Bend the grape spray stem back to
touch the back of the angel's head.

7. Clip the stems from the holly leaves.
Glue the leaves under angel's chin.

8. Make a 3-inch bow from the 18-inch
length of ribbon. Glue the bow under
the angel's chin on top of the holly
leaves.

9. Slip one end of the 8-inch length of
ribbon through the loop made from
the stem. Fold the ribbon in half and tie
an overhand knot ½ inch from the
open end.

DOVE OF PEACE

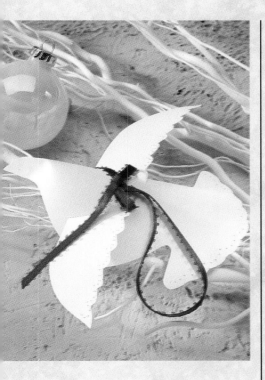

1. Cut out all patterns. See page 63 for the "Dove of Peace" patterns. See Introduction, page 5, for directions on cutting out patterns.

2. Trace the patterns on drawing paper.

3. Cut out the bird and wings with scissors and craft knife.

4. Slice slits for the wings (indicated on the pattern).

5. On the backside of the paper, draw a line about ⅛ inch in from the edge that follows the outline of the wings and tail.

6. Following the lines, poke a pinhole through the paper every ⅛ inch.

7. Fold ½ inch of the bird's head together, matching the beaks. Bond the head together using rubber cement.

8. Poke a pinhole through the paper at the eye mark (indicated on the pattern).

9. Slide the wings through the slits and center.

10. Fold the 8-inch length of ribbon in half. Glue the open end to the bird's body above the shoulders (indicated on the pattern).

11. Make a 1-inch bow from the 12-inch length of ribbon.

12. Glue the bow over the ends of the 8-inch length of ribbon.

CHILDREN'S THEME TREE

❧

*Your young ones will
absolutely love
the clever ornaments
you make to decorate
a theme tree
just for children.
Dinosaurs, teddy bears,
and snowmen
will prance about
your tree on
Christmas morning. Be
sure to see the
Introduction for
some great suggestions
for Children's tree skirts,
garlands, and toppers.*

Pom-Pom Snowman

What You'll Need

2½-inch pom-pom

2-inch pom-pom

1-inch pom-pom

Hot glue mini gun

⅝-inch top hat

3½-inch broom

8-inch striped knit scarf,
⅞ inch wide

½-inch plastic carrot

Wire cutters

2 goggle eyes, 4 mm each

3 black buttons, 4 mm each

White craft glue

Tweezers

8 inches white ⅛-inch ribbon

1. Pushing acrylic puff aside, find the center of the 2½-inch and 2-inch pom-poms. Glue centers together with hot glue. Attach the 1-inch pom-pom to the 2-inch pom-pom in the same manner and in line with the 2½-inch pom-pom, forming a "snowman."

2. Apply hot glue to the underside of the top hat; attach to the top of the 1-inch pom-pom.

3. Lay the broom diagonally across the snowman with the upper end touching the underside of the hat's brim. Hot glue the upper end of the broom to the underside of the hat's brim. Let dry.

4. Using hot glue, attach the lower part of the broom to the bottom pom-pom.

5. Fold the striped scarf in half lengthwise. Insert the scarf through the space between the head and the broom. Knot the scarf at the side of the head. Unfold scarf ends.

6. Snip off the carrot top. Apply hot glue to the carrot's end and place for the snowman's nose.

7. Using white glue and tweezers, place the snowman's eyes and buttons.

8. Fold the ribbon in half; make an overhand knot ½ inch from the open end. Using hot glue, attach the folded half to the center top of the top hat.

4. Place the pattern for the main figure on the bright yellow felt.

5. Trace the general shape of the figure at least ½ inch beyond the figure.

6. Following the traced lines, cut out the general shape. This will serve as the backing.

7. Unfold one thickness of batting. Trace the pattern of the main figure on the batting.

8. Move ¼ inch inside the traced pattern and redraw the pattern.

9. Cut out the figure, following the inner traced line.

WHAT YOU'LL NEED

Scissors
Felt squares: bright blue and bright yellow
Pen or pencil
Polyester craft batting
White craft glue
6-mm goggle eye
10 inches gold thread
Needle

1. Cut out all patterns. See page 61 for the "Dinosaur in December" patterns. See Introduction, page 5, for directions on cutting out patterns.

2. Place the pattern for the main figure on the blue felt square. Trace the pattern with a pen or pencil.

3. Following the traced lines, cut out the figure. The side with the tracing lines will be called the wrong side.

10. Place the batting on top of the wrong side of the blue felt. (There should be about a ¼-inch space between the edge of the batting and the edge of the figure.) Run a thin line of craft glue at the edge of the figure.

11. Pick up the figure and batting; be sure not to touch the glue or let the batting slip. Place the figure and batting on top of the backing material (the yellow felt). Press the edges of the figure onto the backing until the glue sets and the figure sticks to the backing. Set aside until the glue dries (about 20 minutes).

12. Trim the backing material to within ⅛ inch of the figure. However, leave extra backing along the spine; slightly scallop this section.

13. Cut out different-size triangular shapes from the yellow felt. These will serve as trim.

14. Fold the triangles in half and cut a nip out of the bottom of the triangles. Open flat.

15. In a random arrangement, glue the triangles to the dinosaur's front.

16. Glue the goggle eye in place for the dinosaur's eye.

17. Thread the needle with the gold thread.

18. Draw the needle through the dinosaur's spine (through both pieces of felt) in the middle.

19. Tie an overhand knot about 4 inches above the figure. Cut off any excess thread.

TIPS AND VARIATIONS

Trace the pattern on a ¼-inch-thick piece of basswood; use a scroll saw to cut out the figure. Decorate with acrylic paints.

Instead of glue, use a fancy stitch in a contrasting color to sew the figure to the backing.

BEARS ON A SLEIGH RIDE

WHAT YOU'LL NEED

4½-inch sleigh
½-inch brush
Red enamel paint
Red oak stain
Assorted bears:
2 pandas, 1½ inches each
1¼-inch koala
2 sitting whites, 1 inch each
1-inch sitting dark brown
1¾-inch standing teddy
1½-inch sitting teddy
3 dark browns, ¾ inch each
Hot glue mini gun
5 candy canes, ⅝ inch each
10 inches tricolor 4-mm cord
5 inches tricolor 4-mm cord
Wire cutters
2 holly leaves, ½-inch leaves
⅛-inch stamen
2 inches red ⅛-inch ribbon
1-inch sisal wreath
White craft glue
Frosted glitter

1. Paint the carriage section (inside, outside, and underneath) of the sleigh red.

2. Stain the runners.

3. Starting at the left rear of the sleigh, hot glue the bears in place in the following counterclockwise order: standing teddy*, koala*, panda, sitting teddy*, sitting dark brown, panda*, and sitting white*. Be sure to vary the direction the bears face. Glue the other sitting white* in the center of the sleigh facing front.

4. Glue the three smaller dark brown bears wherever there is a hole in the bear arrangement.

5. Using hot glue, attach a candy cane to the left paw of all asterisked (*) bears.

6. Sear the ends of the tricolor cords to prevent unraveling.

7. Using hot glue, attach one end of the 10-inch length of tricolor cord to the sleigh's front; attach the other end to the sleigh's rear.

8. Make a 2-inch bow from the 5-inch length of cord. Using hot glue, attach the bow to the sleigh's front to cover the end of the 10-inch length of cord.

9. Trim the stems from the holly leaves. Attach above the bow, using hot glue. Trim the stem from the stamen and attach where holly leaves touch, using hot glue.

10. Make a 1-inch bow from the 2-inch length of red ⅛-inch ribbon. Some sisal wreaths come with a felt bow. If your wreath has a bow, remove it. In its place, attach the 1-inch bow using hot glue.

11. Using hot glue, attach the wreath to the sleigh's rear to cover the end of the 10-inch length of cord.

12. Spread white glue over the tops of runners, the top edge of the sleigh, the tops of the bears' heads, and the top of the wreath. Sprinkle on frosted glitter.

TIPS AND VARIATIONS

Craft stores generally carry a wide assortment of animals. Fill the sleigh with your personal favorites.

If you cannot find tiny dark brown bears, use ½-inch prewrapped packages.

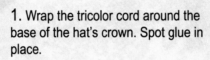

WHAT YOU'LL NEED

4-inch sombrero
8 inches tricolor 3-mm cord
Hot glue mini gun
Wire cutters
¾-inch glazed holly leaf pick
2 red stamens, ⅛ inch each
6-mm jingle bell
3 plaid stockings, 1½ inches each
3 Santa hats, ¾ inch each
8 inches gold elastic cord

1. Wrap the tricolor cord around the base of the hat's crown. Spot glue in place.

2. Trim the ends of the cord at an angle. Apply a dab of glue to each end to prevent unraveling. Glue the ends to the edge of the brim.

3. Take apart the holly pick and trim the stems from the leaves. Glue in place where the cord overlaps at the crown's base.

4. Glue the stamens onto each holly leaf. Glue the bell where cord overlaps at the crown's base.

5. Turn the hat over. Glue the Santa hats and plaid stockings at the edge of the hat's brim. The hats and stockings should alternate and be evenly spaced.

6. Turn hat upright. Fold the gold cord in half. Tie an overhand knot ½ inch from the open end. Glue the folded end to the top center of the crown.

NOEL ROCKING HORSE

WHAT YOU'LL NEED

3-inch embroidery frame
Walnut stain
½-inch brush
5-inch-square muslin
Scissors
Hot glue mini gun
10 inches green ½-inch eyelet
5 inches red ¼-inch looped ribbon
8 inches red ¼-inch looped ribbon
3-inch rocking horse
Acrylic paints: white, red, green, and yellow
5/0 red sable brush

1. Using ½-inch brush, stain embroidery frame.

2. Stretch the muslin in the frame. Trim any excess material.

3. Glue eyelet to the back of the frame; overlap the eyelet's ends.

4. Make a 1-inch bow from the 5-inch length of ribbon. Glue to the top of the frame to cover the space in the outer frame.

5. Insert the 8-inch length of ribbon through the gap in the frame hardware. Tie an overhand knot ½ inch from the open end.

6. Paint the horse's mane white. Let dry. Paint the horse's body red. Let dry. If necessary, give a second coat.

7. Paint the rocker green. Let dry. Paint the saddle green. Let dry. If necessary, give a second coat. (The horse's ears and the tips of the rocker will overhang the frame. Be sure to paint the back of the figure in these areas. Also remember to paint the edges of the horse.)

8. Paint the mane yellow. Let dry. If necessary, give a second coat.

9. Using the 5/0 brush, add yellow trim to the rocker and saddle areas. Add a green bow and braid to the mane and an eyelid and eyelashes.

10. Glue horse to muslin.

2-inch partridge
Wire cutters
2½-inch bark nest
Hot glue mini gun
8 inches red ⅛-inch ribbon
Moss
24 inches red ¼-inch looped ribbon
6 inches red ¼-inch looped ribbon

1. Snip the wire from the bird's feet.

2. Glue the bird into the nest's opening.

3. Thread the 8-inch length of ribbon through the hook at the top of the nest. Tie an overhand knot ½ inch from the ends.

4. Arrange and glue the moss around the hook and ribbon.

5. Make a 2½-inch loopy bow from the 24-inch length of ribbon. Tie off the bow with the 6-inch length of ribbon.

6. Glue the loopy bow to the moss in front of the hook and ribbon.

Tips and Variations

Instead of moss, sprinkle on crystal glitter to make it look like a snow-covered nest.

Try a different type of bird: cardinal, blue jay, robin, or any other bird that strikes your fancy.

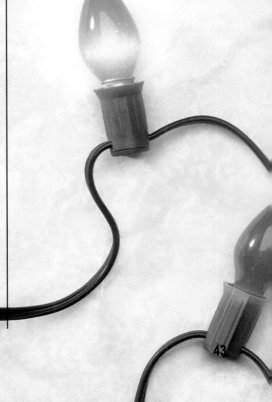

SANTA'S SLEIGH

1. Glue the ¾-inch packages into the sleigh, starting at the right front corner. About ¼ inch to ½ inch of the packages should show above the side of the sleigh.

2. Glue the ½-inch packages into the sleigh, starting at the left front corner. The bottom of the first ½-inch package should sit on the front corner of sleigh.

3. Make a ¾-inch bow from the 3-inch length of red ribbon.

4. Remove the bow that came on the wreath. Glue the ¾-inch bow in its place. Set the wreath aside.

5. Glue the candy canes into the left rear corner of the sleigh.

6. Glue the wreath in front of the candy canes.

7. Glue one end of the 8-inch length of gold cord to the front of the sleigh; glue the other end to the rear of the sleigh.

8. Make two 1-inch bows from the 4-inch lengths of gold cord. Glue one bow at each end of the 8-inch length of gold cord.

WHAT YOU'LL NEED

4-inch wicker sleigh
Hot glue mini gun
3 gift packages, ¾ inch each
2 gift packages, ½ inch each
3 inches red ⅛-inch ribbon
1½-inch sisal wreath
2 candy canes, 2¾ inches each
8 inches gold elastic cord
2 lengths gold elastic cord,
4 inches each

TIPS AND VARIATIONS

*Instead of gift packages,
fill the sleigh with candy,
bears, small flowers,
miniature sports equipment, or
a special gift such as an
engagement ring.*

BRAIDED CANDY CANE 🎄

4. Place 1 length of red ribbon on top of 1 length of white ribbon. Fold in half and glue the ends together. Glue the ends to the top edge of the candy cane.

5. Place the second length of red ribbon on top of the second length of white ribbon. Make a 1½-inch bow and glue over the ends of the other ribbons.

1. Turn up the long edge of one of the strips of calico ¼ inch. Iron flat. Enclose a length of florist wire into the fold. Continue making ¼-inch folds until you have a strip ¼ inch wide by 13 inches long. Clip florist wire that sticks out from the strip. Repeat with the other two strips of material.

2. Braid the three strips together.

TIPS AND VARIATIONS

You can use this same technique to make a wreath.
Use strips that are 18 inches long. After braiding, turn only one end back on itself. Shape the weaving into a circle and glue the unfinished end behind the wreath. Glue a 1-inch eyelet around the outside of the wreath.

WHAT YOU'LL NEED

2 strips red calico, 1½ inches by 13 inches each

1½-inch by 13-inch white with red dots strip of material

Iron

3 lengths covered florist wire, 18 inches each

Wire cutters

Hot glue mini gun

Scissors

2 lengths red ⅛-inch ribbon, 8 inches each

2 lengths white ⅛-inch ribbon, 8 inches each

3. Turn the ends back on themselves and glue in place. Cut off any extra material. Bend into a candy cane shape.

YULETIDE BAUBLE

WHAT YOU'LL NEED

10½ inches tricolor 3-mm rattail cord
4½ inches tricolor 3-mm rattail cord
Matches
3 feet gold 2-mm rattail cord
3 feet red satin 2-mm rattail cord
1 foot gold 2-mm rattail cord
1 foot red satin 2-mm rattail cord
10 inches gold 2-mm rattail cord
White craft glue
1 spray 1-inch red carnations,
12 flowers total
Wire cutters
Hot glue mini gun
2 sprays 3-mm gold balls
Florist tape
2-piece clear plastic 4-inch egg
23-inch string 2-mm gold beads
18 gold balls, 9½ mm each
8 gold balls, 12 mm each

1. Sear the ends of the tricolor cord lengths to prevent unraveling. Apply a dab of white glue to the ends of the gold and red cord lengths to prevent unraveling.

2. Trim the bottoms from three carnations; arrange them in a circle. Hot glue the carnations together.

3. Arrange the remaining carnations in a 2½-inch-high spray. Insert a gold ball spray on either side. Bind together with florist tape. Trim stems.

4. Trim the bottoms from the carnation leaves until the leaves are 1½-inches long. Arrange the leaves around the bottom of the carnation spray and attach with hot glue.

5. Insert the carnation and leaf spray into the center of the 3-carnation circle. Hot glue into place.

6. Open the plastic egg. Center the carnation spray in the bottom of the egg half that has the inner lip. Hot glue the spray in place. Close the egg.

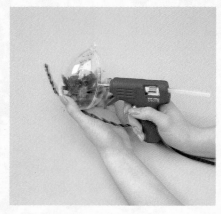

7. Fold the 10½-inch tricolor length of cord in half. Hot glue the middle of the cord to the egg's bottom, covering the egg seam. Using the hot glue gun, spot glue the cord up either side of the egg, covering the egg seam. (The cord will not reach to the egg's top.)

8. Using hot glue, attach one end of the 23-inch string of beads to one end of the tricolor cord near the egg's top. At 6 inches along the bead strand, glue to the other end of the tricolor cord. At 12 inches along the bead strand, glue to the first end of the tricolor cord. At 17½ inches, glue to the second end of the tricolor cord. At 23 inches, glue to the first end of the tricolor cord. You should have a double drape of beads on either side of the egg.

9. Using hot glue, attach the 4½-inch length of tricolor cord around the egg's top, touching but not covering the ends of the tricolor cord covering the egg seam.

10. Using hot glue, attach the 12-mm balls to the egg above the 4½-inch length of tricolor cord.

11. Using hot glue, attach the 9½-mm balls to cover any spaces between the larger balls.

12. Make a 1-inch loopy bow from the 3-foot lengths of red and gold cord. Use the 1-foot lengths of red and gold cord to secure the bow. Attach the loopy bow to the egg's top with an overhand knot, anchor with hot glue. (Use the 1-foot length of red cord that secured the loopy bow to tie the overhand knot.)

13. Insert the 10-inch length of gold cord through the loop at the egg's top. Tie an overhand knot about ½ inch from the open end.

COUNTRY THEME TREE

❧

*Amid the hustle
and bustle of city life,
the call of the countryside
is always enticing.
Reflect a simpler
lifestyle with
country ornaments like
Holiday Holstein and
Old World St. Nick that
will make your hearth
even warmer. Add an
extra touch to your
Country tree by using the
garland, skirt, and topper
suggestions found in the
Introduction.*

HOLIDAY HOLSTEIN

1. Paint the cow with two coats of white paint. Use black paint to place markings on the cow.

2. Glue the heart onto the cow.

3. Thread the bell onto the 3-inch length of ribbon. Glue the ribbon around the cow's neck, attaching at the back of the neck.

4. Make a 1-inch bow from the 4-inch length of ribbon. Glue the bow on top of the 3-inch length of ribbon on heart side of the cow.

5. Fold the 8-inch length of ribbon in half and tie an overhand knot ½ inch from the open end. Glue to the cow's back.

6. Glue the holly leaves and stamens just below the 8-inch piece of ribbon.

WHAT YOU'LL NEED

4-inch cow
½-inch brush
Acrylic paints: white and black
Hot glue mini gun
⅝-inch red heart
⅜-inch cowbell
3 inches red ⅛-inch ribbon
4 inches red ⅛-inch ribbon
8 inches red ⅛-inch ribbon
2 holly leaves, ½-inch leaves
2 stamens, ⅛ inch each

TIPS AND VARIATIONS

If you can't find prepainted red hearts, get unpainted ones and use red enamel paint for a shiny surface.

An encyclopedia will have photographs of many different breeds of cows; choose another breed for a different look.

WHAT YOU'LL NEED

4 inches 7-inch-wide red paper twist
for body

3 inches 7-inch-wide red paper twist
for cape

2¾ inches 7-inch-wide red paper twist
for hood

7 inches 3½-inch-wide brown paper
twist for sack

Hot glue mini gun

Pencil

8 inches gold elastic cord

Wood wool

½-inch-square prewrapped present

2 candy canes, 2 inches each

Two lengths gold elastic cord,
12 inches each

Wire cutters

2 holly leaves, ½-inch leaves

¼-inch jingle bell

15-mm Santa head

1. Untwist and open all paper twist.

SANTA'S BODY:

1. Fold up ½ inch on the 7-inch side of
the 4-inch paper twist. The paper
should now be 3½ inches by 7 inches.
This will be Santa's body. The folded
side will be on the inside and bottom of
Santa.

2. Glue one 3½-inch end over the
other 3½-inch end, forming a 3½-inch
tube (the ½-inch fold should be on the
inside of the tube).

3. Squeeze together one unfolded end
and glue, forming a 3½-inch-high cone.

SANTA'S CAPE:

1. To start making Santa's cape, fold
the 3-inch by 7-inch red paper twist in
half, forming a 3-inch by 3½-inch
rectangle.

2. Make a pencil mark one inch back
from the open 3-inch end on one of the
3½-inch sides.

3. Cut an arc from the pencil mark to
the other corner of the open end.

4. Fold each resulting acute corner
back ¼ inch to form lapel. Glue one
acute corner to the top of the cone that
forms the body. Wrap the cape around
the cone and glue the other acute
corner over the first.

5. Gather the rest of the top of the
cape to the top of the cone and glue to
the cone.

SANTA'S HOOD:

1. Fold the 8-inch length of gold cord
in half. Make an overhand knot ½ inch
from the open end. Put aside.

2. Fold up ¾ inch on the 7-inch side of the 2¾-inch paper twist. The paper should now be 2 inches by 7 inches. This will be Santa's hood. The folded side will be on the outside and at the front of the hood.

3. With the fold on the outside, fold the hood in half.

4. Starting at the closed end and opposite the folded side, cut an arc to the edge of the fold at the open end.

5. Insert the tied gold cord into the closed end opposite the fold; this will serve as the hanger.

6. Glue the hood along the arc.

SANTA'S SACK:
1. To start making Santa's sack, fold the brown paper twist in half, forming a 3½-inch-by-3-inch rectangle. The closed end will be the bottom of the sack.

2. At the closed end, make a pencil mark about 1 inch in from the side. On each side, make a pencil mark about two inches from the closed end.

3. Cut an arc from one mark on the closed end to one mark on the side. Repeat for the other 2 marks. This will be the curved bottom of Santa's sack.

4. Glue the curved sides together and turn the sack inside out.

5. Stuff bag with wood wool.

6. Gather the sack about 1 inch from the top.

7. Glue the prewrapped present in the opening of the sack. Glue the candy canes in place behind the present.

8. Tie the two 12-inch lengths of gold cord around the gathered opening of the sack. Tie a 1-inch bow at the front of the sack.

9. Trim the stems from the holly leaves. Glue the leaves just below the bow.

10. Glue the jingle bell where the holly leaves meet. Set sack aside.

PUTTING IT ALL TOGETHER:

1. Glue Santa's head on top of the cone that forms the body and cape.

2. Glue the hood in place at Santa's neck.

3. Compress and roll a clump of wood wool around in your hands. Form a beard around the bottom of Santa's face and glue into place.

4. Do the same with another clump of wood wool to form Santa's hair. Glue into place.

5. Glue the hood to the top of the hair.

6. Glue the sack, at an angle, to the front of Santa.

COUNTRY CHRISTMAS GOOSE

1. This type of goose often comes with a felt bow on its neck. Carefully remove the felt bow but leave the felt neck band.

2. Cover the felt band with the ¾-inch piece of red ¼-inch ribbon. Fold the 10-inch length of red ⅛-inch ribbon in half. Glue the open end to the ¼-inch ribbon at the back of the neck.

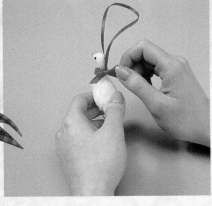

3. Make a 1-inch bow from the 5-inch piece of red ¼-inch ribbon. Glue the bow to the back of the goose's neck on top of the neck band and the ⅛-inch ribbon.

4. Glue one end of the 7-inch length of red-checked ribbon in the center of one side of the bale. Wrap the ribbon around the bale and glue the other end over the first end.

5. Center and wrap the 7-inch piece of ⅛-inch ribbon around the 7-inch checked ribbon. Glue in place.

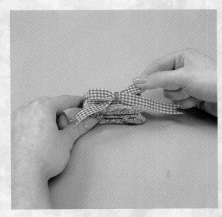

6. Make a 3-inch bow from the 12-inch length of red-checked ribbon. Cover the center knot of the bow with the 1-inch length of ⅛-inch ribbon. Glue the bow to the side of the bale, covering the glued ends of the ribbons wrapped around the bale.

7. Trim the stems from the holly leaves. Glue the leaves into the knot of the bow. Trim the stems from the stamens and glue the stamens onto the holly leaves.

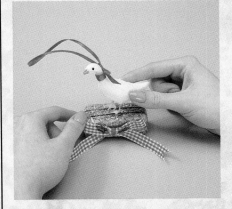

8. Clip the wires protruding from the goose's feet. Glue the feet to the top of the bale; the goose should be turned slightly to the side of the bale with the bow.

WHAT YOU'LL NEED

2 ¾-inch goose
¾ inch red ¼-inch ribbon
Hot glue mini gun
10 inches red ⅛-inch ribbon
5 inches red ¼-inch ribbon
7 inches red-checked ½-inch ribbon
2½-inch bale
7 inches red ⅛-inch ribbon
12 inches red-checked ½-inch ribbon
1 inch red ⅛-inch ribbon
Wire cutters
2 holly leaves, ½-inch leaves
2 stamens, ⅛ inch each

BUTTONS 'N' EYELET WREATH

1. Fold ⅛-inch ribbon in half. Tie an overhand knot ½ inch from the open end. Using the glue gun, glue the folded end to the rear of the wreath.

2. Using the glue gun, glue the eyelet to the back of the wreath. The ends of the eyelet should overlap.

3. Using white glue, arrange the ⅝-inch buttons around the wreath in a random arrangement.

4. Using white glue, arrange the ⅜-inch buttons randomly around the wreath.

WHAT YOU'LL NEED

8 inches eggshell ⅛-inch ribbon
Hot glue mini gun
4-inch grapevine wreath
12 inches eggshell 1-inch eyelet
White craft glue
5 white buttons, ⅝ inch each
20 white buttons, ⅜ inch each

Old-Fashioned Buttermold

1. Make a 2½-inch bow from the ½-inch ribbon. Glue the bow to the top of the buttermold.

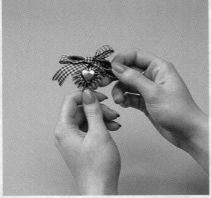

2. Take apart the holly pick and clip stems. Glue the leaves in the knot of the bow. Do the same with the stamens.

3. Make a ¾-inch bow from the ⅛-inch ribbon. Glue to the bottom of the buttermold.

4. Fold the elastic cord in half and tie an overhand knot ½ inch from the open end. Glue the cord to the rear of the 2½-inch bow.

What You'll Need

12 inches blue-checked ½-inch ribbon
Hot glue mini gun
Heart-shaped tin buttermold
3-leaved glazed holly pick,
½-inch leaves
2 stamens, ⅛ inch each
Wire cutters
2 inches blue-checked ⅛-inch ribbon
8 inches gold elastic cord

Tips and Variations

You can find tin buttermolds in cake decorating or candy supply stores. Try a variety of shapes to make a whole series of ornaments.

Jute Twist

1. Bend one spray into an arc with each end pointed left. Bend the other spray into an arc with each end pointed right.

2. Glue the stems of the sprays together.

3. Make a loopy bow from the 3-foot length of jute. Tie the center of the bow with the two lengths of 10-inch jute.

4. Glue the bow to the stems of the sprays.

5. Fold the 8-inch length of jute in half. Glue the open end to the rear of the stems.

What You'll Need

2 red grape sprays,
3½ inches each
Hot glue mini gun
3 feet ⅛-inch jute
2 lengths ⅛-inch jute,
10 inches each
8 inches ⅛-inch jute

Tips and Variations

You can use any color grape you wish. Be sure the spray is three to four inches long; a larger spray may be too heavy for the tree limb.

1. Cut a small hole in the center of the batting. Cut the batting into an uneven circle.

2. Pass the ornament's hanger cord through the hole in batting. Glue the batting into place at the North Pole.

3. Glue the penguin just in front of the hanger cord. Glue the trees to either side of the penguin.

WHAT YOU'LL NEED

Scissors
2-inch square polyester batting
3-inch globe ornament
Hot glue mini gun
¾-inch penguin
2 sisal trees, 2 inches each

TIPS AND VARIATIONS

Instead of a penguin, use a picture of your child. Find a photograph of your child that is about 1½ inches by 2 inches. Using a craft knife, cut your child out from the rest of the photograph. Glue the outline to a thin piece of cardboard. Trim any excess cardboard.

BOUNTIFUL SANTA

WHAT YOU'LL NEED

Scissors

Felt squares: red and black

White craft glue

Foam ball, 3-inch diameter

Sequin pins

Wooden ball, 30-mm diameter

½-inch brush

Acrylic paints: white, black, blue, and red

White craft fur

9 inches red ¹/₁₆-inch ribbon

¼-inch white pom-pom

Hot glue mini gun

5/0 sable brush

2 holly leaves, ½-inch

⅛-inch stamen

Wire cutters

2 candy canes, 2½-inches

10 inches plaid ⅜-inch ribbon

Frosted sisal tree, 3½ inches

GETTING STARTED:

1. Cut out the patterns for "Bountiful Santa." See page 64 for the patterns. See Introduction, page 5, for instructions on cutting out patterns.

2. Following the pattern for Santa's body, cut 7 pieces from the red felt. Apply white craft glue to the foam ball. Attach the felt pieces to the ball and hold in place with pins. The pieces should be evenly distributed around the ball and overlap slightly. After the glue has dried, remove the pins. Set aside.

3. Paint the wooden ball white with the ½-inch brush. Set aside until the paint has dried.

4. From the craft fur, cut the following pieces: 1 circle, 2-inch diameter, for the bottom; 1 belt, 10 inches by ¾ inch; 2

cuffs, 1½ inches by ½ inch each; 1 chest, 2½ inches by ¾ inch; 1 collar, 5 inches by ¾ inch; 1 trim for hat, 6 inches by ½ inch; 1 beard, follow pattern from page 64.

5. Following the pattern, cut 2 mittens and 1 belt buckle from the black felt. Following the pattern, cut 2 arms and 1 hat from the red felt.

SANTA'S HAT:

1. To make Santa's hat, apply white glue to one straight side of the cut red felt. Overlap glued straight side to other straight side, forming a cone.

2. Using white glue, attach the trim for the hat to the bottom edge of the cone.

3. Fold the red ribbon in half. Insert the open end into the top of the cone. Attach the ribbon in place using white glue.

4. While holding the ribbon along the seam of the hat, use white glue to attach the white pom-pom over the ribbon to the top of the cone. Set aside.

PUTTING IT ALL TOGETHER:

1. Use the white glue to assemble Santa. Glue in the following order: circle to bottom of ball (where the body pieces overlap), belt around middle of ball, mittens to straight ends of arms, cuffs over ends of mittens and arms, rounded ends of arms to either side of top of ball, chest piece from top of ball to belt, and belt buckle to center front of belt.

2. Using hot glue, attach the wooden ball to the top of the foam ball where the body pieces overlap.

3. Fold the collar piece in half to find the middle of the collar. Using white glue, glue the middle of the collar to the back of Santa's head where it joins Santa's body. Place the front points of the collar under Santa's chin.

4. Using white glue, attach Santa's beard.

5. Using white glue, attach Santa's hat. Be sure the hat seam is toward the rear.

6. Using the 5/0 brush and acrylic paints, paint Santa's face as shown.

7. Trim the stems from the holly leaves and stamen. Using white glue, attach the leaves and stamen to Santa's beard beneath his right cheek.

8. Cross the candy canes and glue them together with hot glue. Glue the crossed candy canes to Santa's right mitten with hot glue.

9. Curve the right mitten tip and glue it (with hot glue) to Santa's buckle.

10. Make a 1³/₄-inch bow from the plaid ribbon. Using hot glue, attach the bow to the stem of the tree.

11. Using hot glue, attach the tree to the left side of Santa's belt buckle. Then glue Santa's left mitten tip to the tree's base.

CROSS-STITCH CHRISTMAS

Color key:

Black	310 DMC
Red	321 DMC
White	Blanc Neige DMC
Yellow	742 DMC
Gold	729 DMC
Light Brown	51c Coats
Dark Brown	81b Coats
Pink	948 DMC
Blue	312 DMC
Light Tan	3024 DMC

Stitch count: 33w × 46h
Finished size: 2.36 × 3.29 inches

1. Find the center of the Aida. Starting at the center of the design, using 2 strands, stitch according to the chart. For the candy cane, make the first stitch of the cross-stitch in white and the second stitch in red.

2. When all cross-stitching is done, backstitch around Santa's beard and fur using 1 strand of black. Backstitch around Rudolph's antlers, paws, and tail with 1 strand of dark brown. Backstitch around part of Santa's boot with 1 strand of white. Using 2 strands of blue, make French knots for Santa's eyes. Using 2 strands of black, make French knots for Rudolph's eyes. Using 2 strands of white, stitch snowflakes in long stitches as indicated in the chart.

3. Following the manufacturer's instructions, apply the iron-on backing to the felt. Trim the felt to the size and shape of the cross-stitched area.

4. Fold the 7-inch length of ribbon in half. Place the open end to the top center of the back of the felt piece. Following the instructions of the manufacturer of the iron-on backing, affix the felt to the back of the cross-stitch.

5. Trim the Aida cloth to within ³/₈ inch of the edge of the cross-stitching. Fringe the Aida cloth by pulling threads from all four sides until the edge of the cross-stitching is reached.

6. Make a ³/₄-inch bow from the 5-inch length of ribbon. Glue to the top center of the ornament.

WHAT YOU'LL NEED

7-inch by 8-inch piece 14-count white Aida cloth
6-strand cotton embroidery floss (see color key)
#24 tapestry needle
Iron-on backing
3-inch by 4-inch piece red felt
7 inches red ⅛-inch ribbon
5 inches red ⅛-inch ribbon
White craft glue

DINOSAUR IN DECEMBER

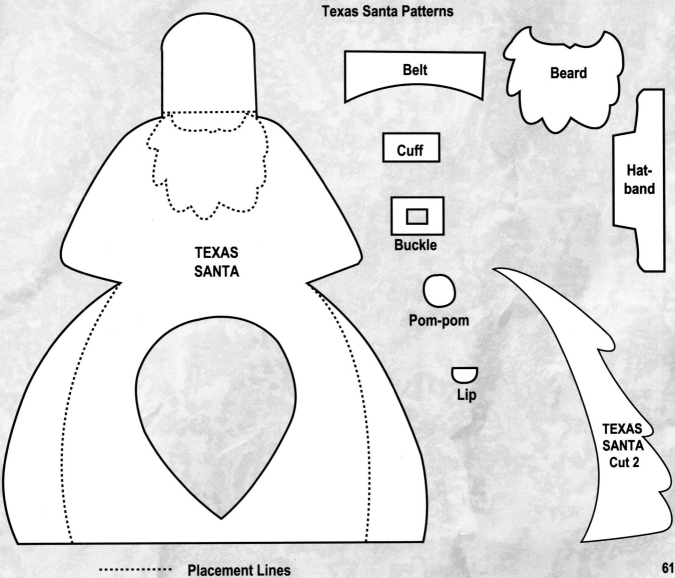

Texas Santa Patterns

Belt

Beard

Cuff

Hat-band

Buckle

TEXAS SANTA

Pom-pom

Lip

TEXAS SANTA Cut 2

- - - - - - - - - **Placement Lines**

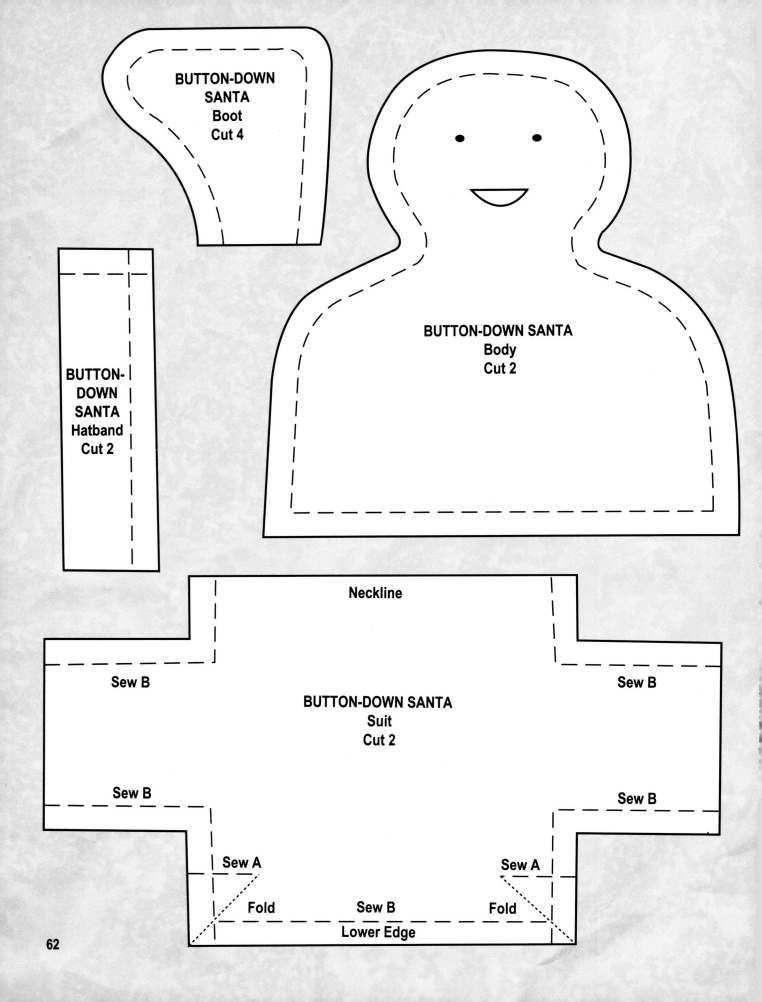

BUTTON-DOWN
SANTA
Boot
Cut 4

BUTTON-
DOWN
SANTA
Hatband
Cut 2

BUTTON-DOWN SANTA
Body
Cut 2

Neckline

Sew B

Sew B

BUTTON-DOWN SANTA
Suit
Cut 2

Sew B

Sew B

Sew A

Sew A

Fold

Sew B

Fold

Lower Edge

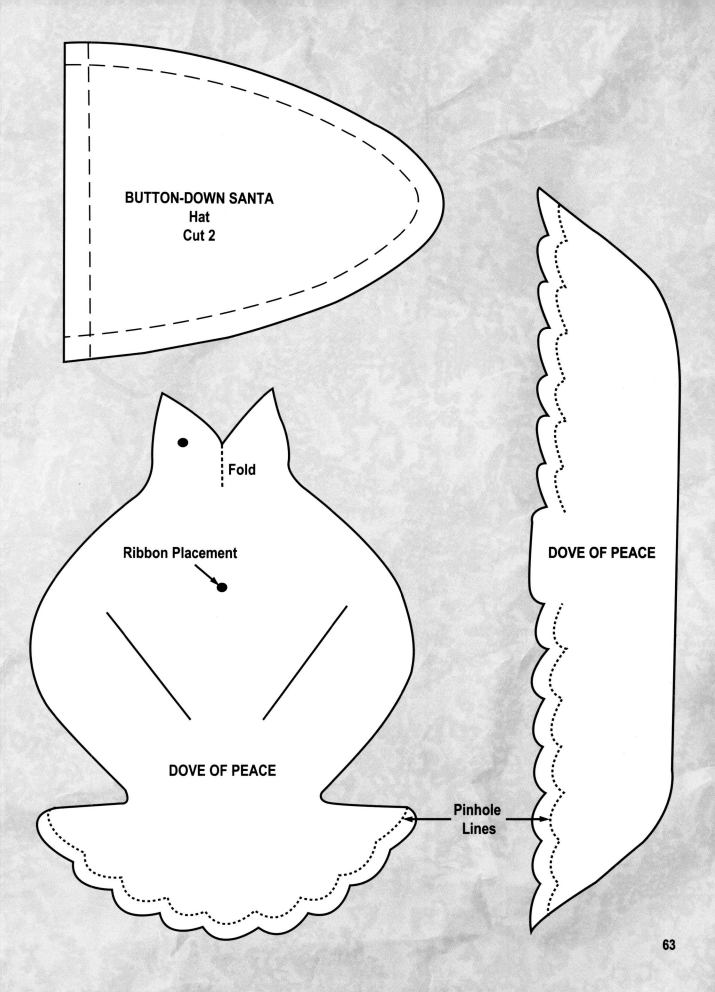

BUTTON-DOWN SANTA
Hat
Cut 2

Fold

Ribbon Placement

DOVE OF PEACE

DOVE OF PEACE

Pinhole
Lines

63

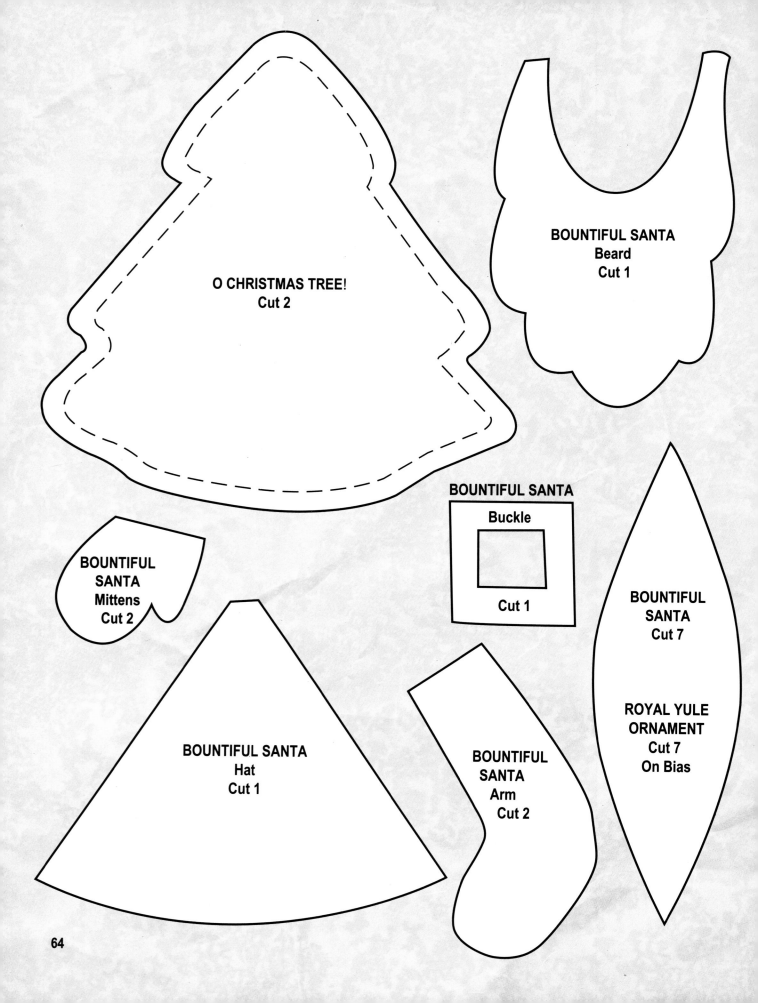

O CHRISTMAS TREE!
Cut 2

BOUNTIFUL SANTA
Beard
Cut 1

BOUNTIFUL SANTA
Buckle
Cut 1

BOUNTIFUL
SANTA
Mittens
Cut 2

BOUNTIFUL
SANTA
Cut 7

ROYAL YULE
ORNAMENT
Cut 7
On Bias

BOUNTIFUL SANTA
Hat
Cut 1

BOUNTIFUL
SANTA
Arm
Cut 2